ONE DROWSY DRAGON

DRAGON

BY ETHAN LONG

Orchard Books · New York
An Imprint of Scholastic Inc.

ONE marching dragon
clanging on a cup.

One drowsy dragon mumbles,
"Don't wake me up!"

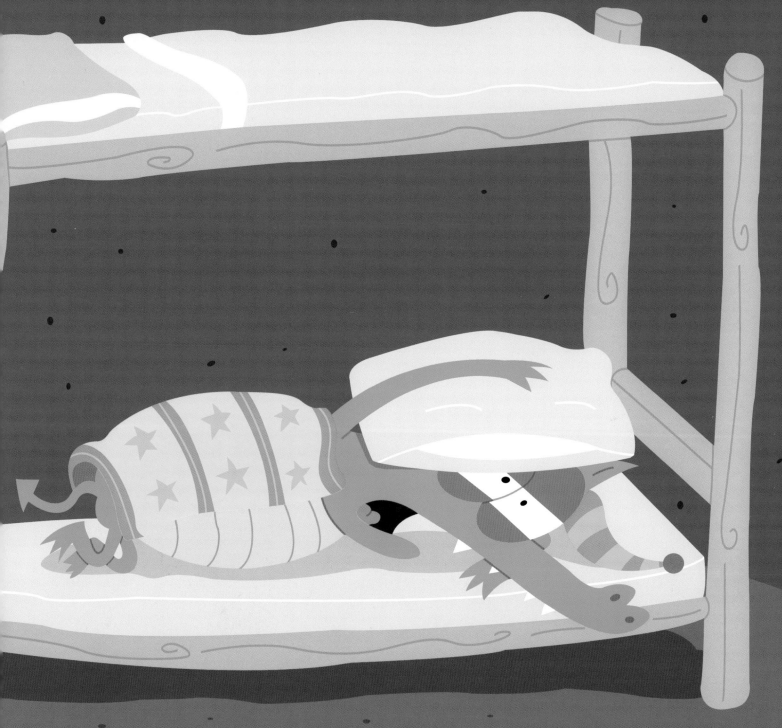

One weary dragon moans,
"Please let me sleep!"

THREE dancing dragons
learn to tap, tap, tap.

One groggy dragon groans,
"I want to nap!"

FOUR feisty dragons
wrestle on the ground.

One tired dragon asks,
"Please keep it down?"

One grumpy dragon hollers,
"Too much noise!"

One mad dragon yells,
"I am still awake!"

SEVEN screaming dragons
watch a scary show.

YIKES!

One loud dragon shouts,
"I'm tired, you know!"

EIGHT rambunctious dragons all play croquet.

One worn dragon shrieks,
"This I cannot stand!"

TEN tuckered dragons
think it's time for bed.

One weary dragon
rests his sleepy head.

One drowsy dragon finally snores deep.

Ten drowsy dragons say...

For Cooper, my idea guy.
Love, Dad — E.L.

Text and illustrations © 2010 by Ethan Long

Library of Congress Cataloging-in-Publication Data is available.
ISBN 978-0-545-16557-0
10 9 8 7 6 5 4 3 2 1   10 11 12 13 14
Printed in Singapore 46 — Reinforced Binding for Library Use — First edition, August 2010
The artwork was created digitally. — The text was set in Bleeker. — Book design by Christopher Stengel